250 QUESTIONS FOR DATES: NEVER ASK ABOUT THE WEATHER AGAIN!

Engaging, Thought Provoking and Fun Prompts to Get the Conversation Started

ALINA NICHOLLS

Silk Publishing

Copyright © 2020 by Silk Publishing

All rights reserved. This book or any portion thereof may not be reproduced or used in any manner whatsoever without the express written permission of the publisher except for the use of brief quotations in a book review.

❧ 1 ☙
PREPARING FOR THE DATE

You dressed up nicely, meticulously chose your outfit, and even made sure to book a reservation at the best restaurant in town. But now, you're sitting across from your date, the silence is becoming too much and it's starting to get awkward because you asked about the *weather*. You don't want to be in that position!

Getting to know someone intimately takes time and thoughtful consideration. That is why asking the right questions is essential in quickly establishing that connection and confirming your compatibility with each other. The goal is to find a common ground, a topic you can both relate to and can comfortably talk about. Once you found that sweet spot, you can totally forget about this list!

That being said, you might as well know whether there are deal-breakers for you that you ought to know right away. Because in that case, it *will* hurt if you don't ask. And with the help of these questions, you won't ever run out of conversation topics again!

2
QUESTIONS

Alright, here are the best questions to ask on your first, second or third date. This is not a list for you to memorize; but to read through, pick your favourites or use as inspiration in coming up with your own topics.

Pro Tip: Underline the questions that resonate with you.

1. What do you like to do in your free time?

2. What movies do you really enjoy?

3. What is the earliest memory you have in life?

4. What is your most bizarre talent?

. . .

5. What is your favorite physical characteristic about yourself?

6. What accomplishments are you proud of?

7. What is something you've always wanted to try but have been too scared to?

8. What is your absolute dream job?

9. What hobbies would you like to get into if you had the time and money?

10. What is the most random thing you've ever watched all the way through on Netflix?

11. What is one thing you wish you had known as freshman in college?

12. What was the last show you binge-watched?

13. What makes you laugh?

14. What is the most romantic thing you have ever done?

. . .

15. What would you do if you had enough money to not need a job?

16. What should I know about you that I'd never think to ask about?

17. What is the one thing in your life that you are not doing that you wish you were?

18. What are you most excited about in life right now?

19. What do you feel people take for granted the most?

20. What's something that comes easier to you that it does for most?

21. What is something about you that would surprise me?

22. What's the best advice anyone has given you?

23. What's something you're interested in that most people wouldn't expect?

24. What nicknames have you had throughout your life?

. . .

25. What do you do differently than most people?

26. What does a typical day look like to you?

27. What does a perfect day look like to you?

28. What do you value most in a friendship?

29. What is your most treasured memory?

30. What is your most terrible memory?

31. What does friendship mean to you?

32. What roles do love and affection play in your life?

33. What should I know about you that I would never think to ask about?

34. What were you like as a kid?

35. What's the weirdest someone has caught you doing?

36. What do you feel most passionate about?

. . .

37. What's something you've been really proud of lately?

38. What is your favorite piece of clothing that you own?

39. What is an automatic deal-breaker for you when pursuing someone in a relationship?

40. What was the worst job you've ever had?

41. What is one skill you wish you could be better at?

42. What do you find most attractive in a potential partner?

43. What are some things everyone should try at least once?

44. What's the best way to get to know who someone really is?

45. What are your guilty pleasures?

46. What has been the most significant plot twist in your own life?

. . .

47. What's currently on your bucket list?

48. What is the hardest you've worked for something?

49. What is your short-term goal right now?

50. What is your long-term goal right now?

51. What are your favorite kinds of food?

52. What is the farthest you have travelled?

53. What is the riskiest adventure you have been on?

54. What's your favorite restaurant?

55. What's your biggest pet peeve?

56. What are you best known for in your family?

57. What is the best and worst thing that has happened to you yet?

58. What is the strangest place you have visited?

. . .

59. What is the most awkward fear you have?

60. What is the most embarrassing thing that has ever happened to you?

61. What is the smallest decision that has had a great impact on your life?

62. What is the strangest place you've ever visited?

63. What is the most bizarre thing someone has ever said to you?

64. What will you say to your younger self if you could go back in time?

65. What is your best and worst flavor of ice cream?

66. What TV shows did you watch as a kid?

67. What do you like to do indoors? How about outdoors?

68. What's your favorite saying?

. . .

69. What's your favorite app on your phone?

70. What's your go-to funny story?

71. What are some of the situations you try to avoid most in life?

72. What do you value most between love and loyalty?

73. What is your ideal spirit animal?

74. What's your favorite cheesy pick-up line? Have you ever used it for real?

75. What is one day you would love to relive?

76. What do you want to be known for?

77. What's the stupidest thing you've ever done for love?

78. What would be a question you'd be afraid to tell the truth on?

79. What is something you wish you did more of in your life and something you wish you did less of?

. . .

80. What is a piece of advice that you were given that if you listened to it, you would not be where you are today?

81. If you only had 30 seconds to share one if the most important things you've learned with the world, what would it be?

82. What's one fear you know is holding you back?

83. What are people often surprised to learn about you?

84. What would you do with the extra time if you never had to sleep?

85. What do you like to eat to cheer yourself up?

86. What is your dream destination?

87. What movie genres do you enjoy watching?

88. What was the last movie that made you cry?

89. What's something you never want your mother to know about you?

. . .

90. What's one character (could be from TV, a movie, or book) you identify with?

91. What would you say is your most redeeming quality?

92. What's your favorite season?

93. What is something you are financially saving up for recently?

94. What's the most spontaneous thing you've ever done?

95. What was your favorite subject in high school?

96. What do you think is the most important life lesson for someone to learn?

97. What do you think is your greatest strength?

98. What was the last dream you had?

99. What is your favorite mistake?

100. What do you think happens to us when we die?

. . .

101. What would your superpower be?

102. What's one thing you cannot live without?

103. What are you known for amongst your friends?

104. What brings you happiness in life?

105. What do you think about modern dating?

106. What's the worst thing you've ever done?

107. What do you think about me so far?

108. What's your point of view in the idea of forever?

109. Who inspires you? Who do you aspire to be like?

110. If you had to spend a year alone with one other person who would it be and why?

111. If you could meet someone who's dead, who would it be and why?

. . .

112. If you could be friends with a celebrity, who would it be and why?

113. If you could switch lives with someone else, who would it be?

114. Who in your family are you closest to?

115. Who is your role model or has had the biggest influence in your life?

116. Who is the most fascinating person you've ever met?

117. Who is your favorite author?

118. Who is your favorite singer/band?

119. Who is your favorite actor/actress?

120. Who's your favorite character from a TV show, movie, or book?

121. Who is the closest person to you?

122. Who would you call if you only had moments to live?

. . .

123. Who was your hero when you were a little kid?

124. When was the last time you sang a song to someone else?

125. When was the last time you dated?

126. When do you mostly demand your personal space?

127. When do you feel most out of place?

128. When you were a kid, what seemed like the best thing about being a grown-up?

129. When do you feel most like yourself?

130. When it comes to love and relationships, what is the first lesson you want to teach your children?

131. When was the last time you did something courageous for yourself?

132. When was the last time life has left you breathless?

. . .

133. When was the last time you cried?

134. When you were younger, what did you want to be when you grow up?

135. When is the right age for you to settle down?

136. Where is your favorite place to go on a weekday afternoon when you have no plans or obligations?

137. Where is your favorite travel get-away?

138. Where is your happy place?

139. Where did you think you'd be when you were little? Are you there now?

140. It's your 75th birthday. Where do you see yourself?

141. If you could live in any fantasy world, where would it be and why?

142. Where would you go on your dream vacation?

143. Where would you go if you were to go on a road trip?

. . .

144. Where would you go if a zombie apocalypse happened right this second?

145. Where do you spend most of your free time?

146. Where have you travelled?

147. If you could live anywhere else in the world, where would it be?

148. Where's the last place you'd ever go?

149. How did you meet your best friend?

150. How many times have you been in love and what did each experience teach you?

151. On a scale of one to ten, how happy are you?

152. How do you celebrate your favorite holiday?

153. How do you unwind?

. . .

154. How do you feel about me?

155. How many dates have you been on before this?

156. In one word, how would you describe yourself?

157. How much social interaction is too much for you?

158. How many siblings do you have?

159. How different do you act when you are with acquaintances versus people you are comfortable with?

160. How have you changed from when you were in high school?

161. Do you believe in supernatural beings?

162. Do you have a sweet tooth or a savory tooth?

163. Do you have any tattoos? What do they mean?

164. Do you prefer hot or cold weather?

. . .

165. Do you consider yourself a morning person or a night owl?

166. Do you have any nicknames?

167. Do you have any special hidden talents?

168. Do you think it's the little things or the grand gestures that matter the most?

169. Do you have any vices?

170. Do you speak any other languages?

171. Do you have any pets?

172. Do you resent your exes or do you wish them well?

173. Do you believe in magic?

174. Do you believe in an afterlife?

175. Do you usually go with your gut or with your brain?

. . .

176. Do you consider yourself to be a good person?

177. Do you think you have a purpose in life?

178. Do you easily get bored?

179. Does anyone know you're on a date right now?

180. Do you prefer indoor or outdoor dates?

181. Do you believe in love at first sight?

182. If you could have any talent, what would it be?

183. If you could change one physical & non-physical thing about yourself, what would it be?

184. If you can only listen to one song, what would it be?

185. If you had one hour left to live, what would you do?

186. If you could come back to life as an animal, what would you be?

. . .

187. If I were to ask your friends about you, what would they say?

188. If you could change one thing about the world, what would it be?

189. If you could travel at any one point in time, when would it be?

190. If you won a million dollars, what would you with it?

191. If you could have a superpower what would you want it to be?

192. If you could erase specific memories from your mind, would you?

193. If you were to open a business, what type of business would you start?

194. If you ruled the world, what would you change?

195. If you could be the opposite sex for one day, what would you do?

196. If you could read minds, how would you use it?

. . .

197. If you can have the answer to any one question, what would it be and why?

198. If you knew you were going to die in a year, what would you change about how you live?

199. If you had all the time and money, what would be your hobbies?

200. For what in your life do you feel most grateful?

201. Do you consider yourself spontaneous, or a planner?

202. Have you ghosted someone before?

203. Which has a higher spot in your priority — relationship or career?

204. How are you going to leave your mark on the world?

205. Would the childhood version of you look up to the current version of you?

206. Do you like what you see when you look in the mirror?

. . .

207. Do you think an animal's life is just as valuable as a human's life?

208. Are you proud to tell people about your job or embarrassed about what you do?

209. Have you ever had your heart broken?

210. Have you ever had a near-death experience?

211. Would you rather be hideous or illiterate?

212. Why do you get up in the morning?

213. Has a song ever made you cry?

214. If aliens came to Earth, would you be scared of them or would you welcome them?

215. Has a book ever changed your life?

216. What is the longest time you could live without your phone?

. . .

217. If you were to be notable for something what would it be?

218. What's one thing you practice on a daily basis that improves your life?

219. What is something you still want to learn?

220. What is your favorite athletic activity?

221. Have you ever lived in another country?

222. What are your principles in life?

223. If you had no fears, what would be the first thing you would do?

224. Do you have a favorite color and why?

225. What is your favorite place you have been to?

226. Which do you prefer, night or day?

227. If you were stranded on an island, what is one item you would take with you?

. . .

228. What was the last book you read?

229. Dogs or cats?

230. What was the stupidest thing you ever spent money on?

231. What would be your superhero name?

232. What's your favorite word?

233. What are you best known for in your family?

234. Are you a religious person?

235. Your favorite non-alcoholic and alcoholic drink?

236. What fact floored you when you heard it?

237. What took you way too long to figure out?

238. What's the hardest you've worked for something?

239. What are you looking forward to that's happening soon?

. . .

240. What's the last new thing you tried?

241. What do you never get tired of?

242. What habit do you wish you could start?

243. What's the most ridiculous thing you've done because you were bored?

244. Where would you like to retire?

245. What's the worst movie you've ever seen?

246. What says the most about a person?

247. What's something that most people haven't done, but you have?

248. What's the luckiest thing that's ever happened to you?

249. What's the best meal you've ever had?

250. What's the most interesting fact you know?

3
KEY TAKEAWAY

So, remember, these questions are to only serve as a guide in navigating your way through the jungle that is dating. Knowing about a potential partner's values, belief system, what makes them tick, and what their day to day life looks like are only some of the things that need to be laid out in the open.

Don't forget that you both are treading unknown waters and chances are, you might not be the only one who's nervous! Understanding this fact may help you handle your composure better. Letting them know that you are might also take some of the pressure off.

And since you're now well-equipped with topics to talk about, you can now relax and have fun!

www.ingramcontent.com/pod-product-compliance
Lightning Source LLC
Chambersburg PA
CBHW020037120526
44589CB00032B/617